TORAH JOHNSON

Veil of Starlight and Desire

Copyright © 2024 by Torah Johnson

All rights reserved. No part of this publication may be reproduced, stored or transmitted in any form or by any means, electronic, mechanical, photocopying, recording, scanning, or otherwise without written permission from the publisher. It is illegal to copy this book, post it to a website, or distribute it by any other means without permission.

This novel is entirely a work of fiction. The names, characters and incidents portrayed in it are the work of the author's imagination. Any resemblance to actual persons, living or dead, events or localities is entirely coincidental.

Torah Johnson asserts the moral right to be identified as the author of this work.

Torah Johnson has no responsibility for the persistence or accuracy of URLs for external or third-party Internet Websites referred to in this publication and does not guarantee that any content on such Websites is, or will remain, accurate or appropriate.

Designations used by companies to distinguish their products are often claimed as trademarks. All brand names and product names used in this book and on its cover are trade names, service marks, trademarks and registered trademarks of their respective owners. The publishers and the book are not associated with any product or vendor mentioned in this book. None of the companies referenced within the book have endorsed the book.

First edition

This book was professionally typeset on Reedsy.
Find out more at reedsy.com

Contents

1	The Arrival of the Stranger	1
2	Secrets of the Veil	7
3	Shadows in the Moonlight	14
4	The Mask of Deception	20
5	Beneath the Silence	25
6	Shadows in the Ballroom	29
7	The Poisoned Truth	33
8	The Flames of Betrayal	38
9	The Forest of Deceit	43
10	The Echoes of Betrayal	48
11	Shadows the Moonlight	54
12	The Heart of Darkness	58

1

The Arrival of the Stranger

The wind carried the scent of salt from the nearby sea, its cool fingers brushing across Lyra's skin as she stood at the edge of the cliff, gazing out at the shimmering ocean beneath the starlit sky. It was a night like any other—or so it seemed. The stars, brilliant and endless, had always fascinated her. She spent most evenings here, where the world felt still, and the sky held more secrets than she could ever comprehend. There was a comfort in their silence, a familiarity in their distant light. But tonight, something felt different. The air was heavier, and there was a weight behind the wind that unsettled her.

She took a deep breath and closed her eyes, trying to shake off the strange feeling. The sound of waves crashing against the rocky shore below normally soothed her, but tonight, the rhythm was off—like something was out of place. Her fingers idly toyed with the pendant hanging from her neck, an old keepsake her grandmother had passed down to her, a delicate silver star that glimmered faintly in the moonlight.

She was about to turn back towards the path that led to her small cottage when she heard the unmistakable sound of footsteps behind her. They were deliberate, slow, yet heavy, as though each step was meant to announce the presence of someone who did not care to hide.

Lyra stiffened, her heart skipping a beat. This part of the cliffs was remote; hardly anyone ventured out here after dark. She wasn't expecting anyone, least of all a visitor. Slowly, she turned, her gaze falling on the figure that now stood several feet away, partially shrouded in shadow.

The man was tall, his silhouette striking against the pale light of the moon. His coat, long and dark, whipped slightly in the wind, and his face remained obscured by the low brim of a hat. He didn't move closer, but there was something about the way he stood—composed, almost too still—that sent a chill down her spine.

"Are you lost?" she asked, her voice more steady than she felt. Her eyes remained locked on him, every muscle in her body tensed.

For a moment, he didn't respond. The silence between them stretched, heavy and suffocating, before he finally spoke.

"No," he replied, his voice deep and smooth, though there was something unreadable in it. "I'm exactly where I'm meant to be."

A sense of unease washed over her at his words. There was something odd about his tone, as if he knew something she didn't. The wind picked up again, stronger this time, swirling around them, carrying a sense of foreboding that made her stomach tighten.

"I've never seen you here before," she said, taking a cautious step back, her eyes flicking towards the path that led to the safety of her home.

The man raised his head slightly, revealing part of his face. His features were sharp, angular, with dark eyes that seemed to glint in the moonlight, though they were devoid of warmth. They bore into her, as if trying to see through her, to unravel her thoughts.

"Perhaps because I wasn't meant to be seen until now," he said softly, his lips curling into a faint, almost amused smile.

Her fingers tightened around the pendant at her throat, the silver star suddenly feeling cold against her skin. "What do you want?"

His smile faded, and his gaze softened, but only slightly. "I'm not here to harm you, if that's what you fear." He took a step forward, slow, deliberate. "I've come to deliver a message."

A message? Her mind raced. From who? And why her?

She took another step back, her instincts screaming at her to run, but curiosity kept her rooted to the spot. "A message? From whom?"

The man's eyes never left hers. "From the stars."

The words hung in the air like a tangible force, making her chest tighten with a mix of fear and disbelief. She felt the weight of his gaze, and for the briefest moment, she thought she saw a flicker of something—something otherworldly—in his eyes.

"The stars don't send messages," she replied, though her voice lacked conviction.

"Don't they?" he asked, tilting his head slightly, his dark eyes glimmering with something she couldn't quite place. "You, of all people, should know better than to dismiss the mysteries of the night."

Her breath caught in her throat. How could he know about her connection to the stars, her late-night vigils under their light, or the dreams that had plagued her recently—dreams filled with voices, whispers, and images she couldn't understand?

"Who are you?" she asked, her voice barely a whisper now, fear tightening its grip around her.

The man took one last step toward her, closing the distance between them. He leaned in just enough for her to see the full depth of his piercing gaze, and for the first time, Lyra felt truly exposed under the weight of it.

"My name is Kieran," he said, his voice low and steady. "And I've been waiting a long time for you, Lyra."

The world seemed to tilt beneath her feet as his words struck her like a blow. He knew her name.

"How…how do you know me?" she stammered, her mind racing.

His lips curled into a faint smile, one that didn't reach his eyes. "The stars have always known you, Lyra. And now, they've sent me to you."

Before she could respond, a gust of wind howled through the cliffs, and the light of the stars above seemed to pulse, as if echoing his words. The veil between what was real and what wasn't seemed to thin, and Lyra, for the first time in her life, felt as though the stars were watching her—really watching.

And the stranger before her wasn't just a man. He was something more, something dangerous.

And he had come for her Lyra's heart pounded in her chest, her instincts urging her to run, but her feet remained frozen in place. The pull she felt toward this man—this stranger who claimed to know her—was undeniable. His presence seemed to warp the very air around them, creating a tension that left her breathless.

"What do you mean, the stars sent you?" she asked, her voice trembling as she forced the words out. "What do they want with me?"

Kieran's eyes flicked upward, towards the sky, the stars reflected in his dark irises. "They want what they have always wanted," he said, his voice low and cryptic. "Balance. Harmony. A future that hangs by a thread."

Lyra shook her head, frustration and fear warring inside her. "You're not making any sense," she whispered, backing up another step. "This… this is insane."

Kieran's gaze dropped back to her, his expression softening slightly. "It's not insane, Lyra. You've felt it, haven't you? The stars… they've always been more than distant lights to you. You've felt their pull, heard their whispers."

She opened her mouth to deny it, to claim that everything he was saying was madness. But she couldn't. Because he was right. For as long as she could remember, she had been drawn to the night sky in a way she could never fully explain. There were times she had felt as though the stars were speaking to her, calling her, though she had always dismissed it as nothing more than an overactive imagination.

"How do you know that?" she asked, her voice barely a whisper now, as if speaking too loudly would break the fragile web of reality they stood within.

Kieran stepped closer, and this time, she didn't move away. "Because I've been watching you, waiting for the moment you would be ready."

"Ready for what?" Lyra demanded, a surge of anger rising in her. "I don't even know you!"

Kieran's expression darkened, his eyes narrowing slightly as if considering how much to reveal. "Ready to accept who you really are. Ready to understand the power that's been dormant inside you for so long."

Lyra's breath caught in her throat. "What are you talking about?"

He raised a hand, and for a moment, she flinched, expecting him to touch her. But instead, his fingers hovered just above her chest, over the pendant that hung around her neck. "This," he said softly, "is not just a trinket. It's a key. A key to a world you've only glimpsed in your dreams."

Lyra glanced down at the pendant, her fingers automatically closing around it protectively. "My grandmother gave this to me," she said, her voice shaking. "It's just a family heirloom."

Kieran's eyes softened, but there was an urgency behind them now, something that told her time was running out. "Your grandmother knew more than she ever told you. This pendant is part of an ancient bond, a connection between your world and the one beyond the stars."

Lyra stared at him, her mind reeling. She wanted to deny everything he was saying, to insist that this was all some elaborate trick. But deep down, she knew. She had always known that there was something more to her grandmother's stories, something she had never fully understood.

"And what does that have to do with me?" she asked, her voice barely audible over the wind.

Kieran's expression grew even more serious, his gaze locking onto hers with an intensity that made her heart race. "Because you are the last of your line, Lyra. The last one who can open the veil between worlds. And there are forces—dark, dangerous forces—that will stop at nothing to prevent that from happening."

2

Secrets of the Veil

Lyra's mind spun as she hurried back down the winding path from the cliffs, the pendant feeling impossibly heavy against her chest. Kieran's words echoed in her head, louder than the sound of the crashing waves below. You are the last of your line. The last one who can open the veil between worlds.

None of it made sense. How could she, a simple girl from a quiet coastal town, be connected to some ancient power? The stars weren't alive, they weren't trying to communicate. And yet… she had always felt their pull, as if something within her resonated with the vastness above.

Her grandmother's stories came flooding back to her—the tales of star-crossed realms, of a veil separating their world from another. As a child, she had listened in wonder, but they were just stories. Weren't they?

The old lighthouse loomed ahead, a solitary structure perched on the rocky shore. Its light had been extinguished long ago, but Lyra often found herself drawn to it, especially on nights like this. It was abandoned, crumbling in places, but the tower held an eerie beauty beneath the starlight. And tonight, after what Kieran had told her, the lighthouse called to her even more urgently.

Lyra reached the entrance, her hand shaking slightly as she pushed open the rusted door. It creaked loudly, the sound echoing through the empty chamber as she stepped inside. The air was damp and musty, thick with the scent of seawater and decay. Faint moonlight filtered through cracks in the stone walls, casting long shadows that made her heart race.

She paused in the center of the room, taking a deep breath to steady herself. The pendant around her neck seemed to hum with energy, as though reacting to the place. She wrapped her fingers around it, feeling the smooth, cold surface against her palm.

This pendant is part of an ancient bond... a connection between your world and the one beyond the stars.

The words stirred something deep inside her, something she couldn't explain. Lyra looked around the room, her eyes scanning the faded walls and broken furniture. Something about the place felt... alive. As if it were waiting.

She approached the base of the spiral staircase that led to the top of the tower. She had climbed it countless times before, to look out over the sea and sky, to think, to breathe. But tonight, as she set foot on the first step, a shiver ran down her spine. The air seemed thicker here, and she had the sudden sensation that she wasn't alone.

Her hand slid along the cool railing as she ascended, the ancient wood creaking beneath her weight. She could hear the wind whistling through the cracks in the tower, but it felt distant now, muffled. Each step she took felt heavier, as though the tower itself resisted her ascent.

Halfway up, she stopped. Her heart pounded in her chest, but it wasn't from exertion. Something was different. She glanced over her shoulder, half-expecting to see Kieran's shadowy figure lurking behind her. But the staircase was empty.

"Pull yourself together," she muttered under her breath, her voice barely a whisper in the silence.

But the sense of being watched didn't fade.

She reached the top, her breath catching as she stepped into the small circular room that crowned the tower. The large, broken window that faced the ocean allowed the night breeze to flow in freely, carrying the scent of salt and seaweed. The stars above seemed brighter here, closer somehow, as if the very tower reached up to touch them.

Lyra crossed the room, her eyes drawn to the old, worn table that stood in the center. She had seen it before—an unremarkable piece of furniture, its surface covered in dust and the remnants of time. But tonight, something caught her eye. The dust had been disturbed, revealing an intricate pattern carved into the wood that she had never noticed before.

Frowning, she knelt beside the table, tracing her fingers over the design. It was a series of swirling lines, almost like constellations, but they didn't match any stars she recognized. Her hand stilled as she reached the center of the pattern, where a small, circular indentation had been carved into the wood.

Her pendant seemed to vibrate against her chest, and a realization struck her.

Without thinking, Lyra unclasped the necklace and carefully lowered the pendant into the indentation. It fit perfectly, as though the table had been made for it. The moment the pendant clicked into place, the air in the room shifted.

The temperature dropped, and Lyra felt a sudden pressure, as if the atmosphere itself had thickened. Her breath hitched, her heart thundering in her chest as a soft glow began

Lyra stood frozen in the lighthouse chamber, her breath shallow and her pulse roaring in her ears. She blinked, trying to ground herself, but the images from the veil swam before her eyes—those figures, the eerie glow, the sense that something vast and ancient had just brushed against her soul. Her hand still tingled where she had touched the veil, as if an electric current lingered just beneath her skin.

What was that? Her mind was racing, trying to make sense of the impossible. The veil, the visions, Kieran's cryptic warnings—it was all too much, too fast. She staggered back from the table, her eyes fixed on the pendant as if it might spring to life again at any moment.

The lighthouse, which had always been her sanctuary, now felt stifling, its silence pressing down on her like a physical weight. She needed to get out, to breathe, to think. Grabbing the pendant from the table, she quickly fastened it back around her neck, the cool metal burning against her skin with an intensity that hadn't been there before.

Lyra turned and hurried down the winding staircase, her footsteps echoing in the narrow passage. Every creak of the old wood seemed amplified, making her flinch as if someone—or something—were following her. The suffocating weight of the air seemed to throb with invisible tension, growing heavier with each step she took.

As she reached the base of the lighthouse and pushed the door open, the night greeted her with an icy gust of wind. She inhaled deeply, filling her lungs with the sharp, salty air, but it did little to ease the tightness in her chest. The stars twinkled innocently above, as if mocking her with their familiar glow. She cast a wary glance up at them, half-expecting to see something unnatural lurking behind their light.

But the sky was still.

Her legs carried her away from the lighthouse and toward the cliff's edge, the same place she had stood just hours before, when everything had been… normal. She felt foolish now, as if the stars had been laughing at her all along, knowing she was on the precipice of something she could never have imagined.

The wind whipped her hair around her face, but she didn't care. Her thoughts churned with too many questions. Why her? Why now? What had she seen beyond that veil? And who were the figures—those shadowy beings that had reached out for her, pulling at her consciousness as though they recognized her?

Kieran's words haunted her. *The stars have always known you, Lyra.* He had spoken with a certainty that unnerved her. She didn't know him, yet something in his voice had struck a chord deep inside her, something she had tried to ignore for too long.

She shook her head. This was madness. She was an ordinary woman, leading an ordinary life. The stars didn't have plans for her. The idea of being part of some ancient legacy, of holding the key to a veil between worlds, was absurd. And yet… the visions had been so real. The veil had been real.

"Lyra."

Her heart stopped. The voice came from behind her, low and smooth, just as it had been on the cliffs. She spun around, her pulse racing, and found Kieran standing a few feet away, his dark coat rippling in the wind. He was even more imposing in the moonlight, his eyes catching the faint glow of the stars.

"I told you not to follow me," she said, her voice sharper than she had intended.

"I didn't follow you," he replied calmly, stepping closer but keeping a respectful distance. "I needed to make sure you were safe."

"Safe?" she scoffed, her frustration bubbling to the surface. "You call this safe? I don't even know what's happening to me. You talk about veils and stars and ancient bonds, but you haven't told me anything that makes sense."

Kieran's gaze softened slightly, but there was still that unshakable intensity in his eyes. "I told you enough to prepare you. I knew the lighthouse would call to you tonight. It was time."

"Time for what?" Lyra's voice cracked with the weight of the questions she hadn't dared to voice. "What's happening to me? Why can I see… things? Why did the veil appear?"

Kieran stepped closer, his expression unreadable. "Because the veil is weakening. The world you saw through it is closer than it has been in centuries. And you, Lyra, are the one who can either open it… or seal it forever."

Her breath hitched. "Seal it? What are you talking about?"

"The figures you saw—what did they look like?" he asked, his tone growing more urgent. "The ones on the other side of the veil. Did they try to reach you?"

Lyra hesitated, flashes of the shadowy forms resurfacing in her mind. Their vague, twisting shapes, the way they had reached toward her, their silent cries that she could feel rather than hear. "Yes," she whispered, her throat tightening. "They… they were calling to me."

Kieran's jaw tightened. "Then it's worse than I thought. The veil isn't just weakening—it's being torn open from the other side."

Lyra's heart pounded in her chest. "Torn open? By what?"

Kieran's gaze darkened, and for the first time since she'd met him, Lyra saw a flicker of fear in his eyes. "There are forces beyond this world, Lyra. Dark forces that have been waiting for centuries to break through. The veil has kept them at bay, but if they succeed in opening it, they'll consume everything—our world, their world—everything."

Lyra felt the ground sway beneath her feet, her pulse a deafening roar in her ears. "Why me?" she asked, her voice small, desperate. "Why do I have anything to do with this?"

"Because you are the key," Kieran said softly. "The bloodline you carry is tied to the stars themselves. You were born with the power to control the veil, whether you want it or not."

Lyra stared at him, her mind struggling to grasp the enormity of what he was saying. "I don't understand."

"You will," Kieran said, stepping closer until he was mere inches from her. His voice dropped to a near-whisper. "But you must choose, Lyra. Do you want to open the veil and face what lies beyond? Or will you help me seal it, once and for all?"

The weight of his words hung between them, the stars above silent and watchful.

Lyra's pulse thundered in her ears, and for the first time, she truly understood: her life, as she had known it, was over. There was no going back.

And the choice before her could shape the fate of the world.

3

Shadows in the Moonlight

The night air was thick with anticipation, the sky veiled by low-hanging clouds that blotted out the stars. Elara could feel the weight of the evening pressing down on her as she stepped cautiously onto the stone path leading away from the estate. Every sound was magnified—the rustle of the wind through the trees, the crunch of gravel beneath her feet, the distant hoot of an owl. She wrapped her cloak tighter around her shoulders, more for comfort than warmth, as a gnawing feeling of dread clawed at her insides.

She shouldn't be out here. Not now. Not like this.

The conversation she had overheard earlier that day echoed in her mind, swirling like a dark mist she couldn't escape. A plot against the duke, whispered by voices too low to be recognized, but the message had been unmistakable. Someone was planning to betray him.

Elara had spent the entire afternoon weighing her options. She could stay quiet, pretend she had heard nothing. After all, it wasn't her fight. But the image of the duke, standing tall with his piercing gaze fixed on her during their brief encounter in the garden a few weeks ago, lingered in her memory. There was something about him—his unspoken sorrow, the way his lips curled slightly at the edges when he wasn't aware of being watched—that made her heart twist unexpectedly.

And so, here she was, following the path that led to the secluded grove where she was supposed to meet the only person she could think to trust. She hadn't seen him in years, not since they were children playing by the riverbanks, but she knew he would be here. He had to be.

The sound of footsteps made her stop, her breath catching in her throat. She crouched low behind a thicket of bushes, her pulse quickening. The footsteps were slow, deliberate, drawing closer with each passing second. She strained her ears, trying to identify the source, but the darkness around her was thick and impenetrable. Elara held her breath, waiting.

A shadow emerged, its form barely distinguishable in the pale moonlight that managed to slip through a break in the clouds. It was tall, lean, and moved with a predatory grace that sent shivers down her spine. The figure paused, mere feet from where she crouched, and for a terrifying moment, Elara thought they had seen her. She could hear her own heartbeat pounding in her ears, her chest tight with fear.

But the shadow moved on, disappearing into the woods with barely a sound.

Elara waited until the footsteps faded completely before she dared to move. She rose slowly, glancing around to make sure no one else was nearby. She had to be more careful. If anyone caught her out here, especially after what she had overheard, her life would be in danger.

She continued along the path, her pace quicker now, driven by a sense of urgency she couldn't quite explain. The grove was just ahead, hidden beyond a small hill. As she climbed, she thought back to those childhood days when she and Ryland had played here, their laughter filling the air as they chased each other through the trees. Back then, the world had seemed so simple, so safe.

But Ryland wasn't a child anymore. He had grown into a man with secrets of his own, a man who, if the rumors were true, was entangled in affairs far more dangerous than she could imagine. Still, he was the only one who could help her now.

When she reached the top of the hill, the grove stretched out before her, bathed in the ghostly glow of the moon. For a moment, she thought she was alone, but then she saw him. Ryland stood at the edge of the clearing, his back to her, his posture tense. He hadn't changed much, except for the scar that now ran along his jawline, a reminder of the life he led away from the peaceful village they had once called home.

"Elara," he said, his voice low and rough, as though he had been waiting for her all night.

She hesitated for a moment before stepping into the open. "Ryland, I need your help."

He turned slowly, his eyes dark and unreadable as they locked onto hers. For a brief moment, the tension between them crackled like a live wire, their shared history hanging in the air like an unfinished sentence.

"What have you gotten yourself into this time?" His tone was half-amused, half-wary, as though he couldn't quite decide whether to laugh or be concerned.

Elara took a deep breath, her heart still racing from the encounter with the shadowy figure. "It's not me," she said quietly. "It's the duke. Someone's planning to betray him, and I don't know who I can trust."

Ryland's expression hardened, his amusement vanishing. "And you think I'm the one who can fix this?" His voice was edged with something dangerous, a sharpness that made Elara shiver.

"I don't know," she admitted. "But I don't have anyone else."

Ryland was silent for a long moment, his gaze never leaving hers. Then, without a word, he turned and walked toward the trees, disappearing into the shadows.

Elara stood frozen, unsure whether to follow or stay. But then his voice came, low and commanding, from the darkness.

Are you coming or not ?

Elara hesitated, her feet rooted to the spot. The weight of the decision before her seemed heavier than she had anticipated. Ryland had changed—he was no longer the carefree boy she had known. His world was darker now, more dangerous. Could she really trust him? But then again, she had no other choice.

Steeling herself, she stepped forward, following him into the trees. The moonlight barely penetrated the dense canopy overhead, casting deep shadows along the path. The air was thick with the scent of pine and earth, and the quiet rustling of leaves was the only sound, save for the occasional distant call of a night bird.

Ryland moved swiftly and silently, as though he knew every twist and turn of the forest by heart. Elara had to quicken her pace to keep up, her heart still pounding in her chest. She wanted to ask where they were going, but the look on his face earlier had warned her against it. He was taking her somewhere—somewhere secret, she realized. Somewhere he knew they wouldn't be overheard.

After what felt like hours but was likely only minutes, Ryland finally stopped. They had reached a small clearing, hidden deep within the woods. A large, crumbling stone structure stood in the center, half-covered by creeping vines and moss. It looked like an ancient ruin, forgotten by time and hidden from prying eyes.

"What is this place?" Elara asked, her voice barely above a whisper.

"Somewhere safe," Ryland replied without turning around. He strode toward the structure and pushed open a heavy wooden door that creaked in protest. Inside, it was dark, but a faint glow from a hearth in the corner revealed a room furnished with little more than a table, two chairs, and a few scattered belongings. It was clear that this was not a place often visited, yet it had been prepared for their arrival.

Ryland motioned for her to sit. "Talk."

Elara swallowed hard, unsure where to begin. She had spent the entire day rehearsing what she would say, but now, faced with Ryland's intense gaze, the words seemed to slip away from her.

"There's a conspiracy against the duke," she said finally, her voice steadier than she felt. "I overheard a conversation in the estate—someone is planning to betray him, but I don't know who. I… I had to tell someone, and you were the only one I could think of."

Ryland's expression was unreadable. He leaned against the wall, arms crossed, as he listened. "And you thought bringing this to me was a good idea? You must know by now that my loyalties are… complicated."

"I know," Elara admitted, her eyes pleading. "But you know more about this world than I do. You have contacts, information. I don't know who else to turn to."

He studied her in silence for a long moment, the firelight casting sharp shadows across his face. When he spoke again, his voice was low, almost a growl. "If you're telling the truth, then you're in more danger than you realize. Betrayals in the duke's court don't end with simple punishments. People disappear, Elara. Or worse."

Her stomach tightened at his words, but she refused to let fear overwhelm her. "I need to stop this. I can't let them succeed."

Ryland's eyes narrowed, his jaw clenching as if he were debating something within himself. Finally, he pushed off the wall and approached her, his presence looming over her like a storm cloud.

4

The Mask of Deception

The next day dawned gray and heavy, as though the sky itself sensed the tension winding through the corridors of the duke's estate. Elara moved through the grand halls with calculated precision, her mind buzzing with the names Ryland had given her the night before. Each one was a potential traitor, a danger to the duke—and to her. She couldn't trust anyone now, not until she had uncovered the truth.

The weight of her mission pressed down on her as she entered the great hall. The estate was bustling with preparations for the upcoming ball, the annual event where all of the duke's closest allies and rivals would gather under one roof. It was the perfect opportunity for the conspirators to make their move, and Elara had little time to act.

Her footsteps echoed against the polished marble floor as she made her way toward Lady Margot, one of the few names she recognized on Ryland's list. Lady Margot was a fixture at the estate—beautiful, clever, and always smiling sweetly at the duke's side. But beneath that charming facade, Elara had often sensed something darker. Lady Margot's eyes, though always warm, held a flicker of calculation, as if every interaction was part of a larger game.

"Elara, dear," Lady Margot's voice rang out as soon as she caught sight of her, smooth and welcoming. She was dressed in a gown of deep emerald silk, her dark hair cascading in perfect waves over her shoulders. She reached out, her fingers brushing lightly against Elara's arm in a show of camaraderie. "You seem troubled. Is something amiss?"

Elara forced a smile, her heart pounding. She had to be careful, had to move delicately. "Not at all, my lady," she replied, keeping her voice steady. "I've simply been overwhelmed with preparations for the ball. I hope everything is to your liking?"

Lady Margot's eyes glittered, her smile never faltering. "Oh, I'm sure it will be a splendid affair, as always. The duke does know how to throw a celebration."

Elara nodded, feeling the tension coil tighter in her chest. She needed more, something concrete, but pressing too hard could be dangerous. She opted for subtlety. "There's always so much intrigue at these events," she remarked casually, her gaze drifting around the room as servants rushed by, decorating the hall with fresh flowers and tapestries. "I imagine it's quite difficult to keep track of all the… politics."

Lady Margot's smile twitched at the edges, almost imperceptibly, but her eyes never left Elara's. "You've no idea, dear," she said, her voice low and conspiratorial. "In a place like this, one must always stay two steps ahead. You never know who might be plotting behind closed doors."

Elara's stomach churned. Was that a veiled confession? Or simply the casual musings of someone who thrived in the court's endless games? She couldn't be sure, but the unease in her gut only deepened. She needed to find out more, to confirm whether Lady Margot was truly part of the conspiracy or merely playing along with the estate's usual schemes.

Before she could respond, a commotion at the entrance of the hall caught her attention. The grand double doors swung open, and the duke himself strode in, his presence commanding as always. His dark hair, streaked with silver at the temples, framed a face that had seen too many battles, both on the field and in the court. His sharp eyes scanned the room, pausing briefly on Elara before moving on to Lady Margot.

"Margot," the duke called out, his voice smooth but carrying an edge that silenced the room. "I trust you'll ensure everything is perfect for tonight."

Lady Margot inclined her head, her smile softening into something more demure. "Of course, Your Grace. You have nothing to worry about."

The duke's gaze flickered back to Elara, and for a moment, their eyes met. There was something in his expression—a quiet intensity, as if he saw more than he let on. It made her skin prickle, the awareness of how precarious her position was. Did he suspect something? Or was she imagining it?

As the duke turned away and continued speaking with other courtiers, Elara's heart thundered in her chest. She had to get away, to think, to gather her thoughts before she did something reckless. Making a quick excuse to Lady Margot, she slipped out of the hall and into one of the smaller, dimly lit corridors that led deeper into the estate.

The air here was cooler, the noise of the main hall fading behind her. She moved swiftly, her footsteps light on the stone floors. She needed to find Ryland, to share what she had learned—though it wasn't much, the slight shift in Lady Margot's expression had been enough to stir her suspicions.

As she rounded a corner, a figure stepped out from the shadows, blocking her path. Elara's breath caught in her throat, her hand instinctively going to the small dagger she had concealed beneath her cloak.

It was him. The man from the night before, the shadowy figure who had passed by her in the woods. His face was mostly hidden by the hood of his cloak, but his presence was unmistakable—tall, imposing, with an air of silent menace.

"Going somewhere, my lady?" His voice was low and mocking, his lips curling into a smile that didn't reach his eyes.

Elara's pulse raced, but she forced herself to remain calm. "Who are you?" she demanded, her fingers tightening around the hilt of her dagger.

The man chuckled, a dark, humorless sound. "That's not important. What is important is that you stop poking your nose where it doesn't belong."

He took a step closer, and Elara's heart thudded painfully in her chest. She could feel the cold stone of the wall at her back, her escape route cut off. She was trapped.

"What do you want?" she asked, her voice barely above a whisper.

His eyes gleamed in the dim light, and for a moment, the room seemed to close in around her. "You know exactly what I want. Stay out of this, or I'll make sure you regret it."

Before she could respond, he was gone, slipping back into the shadows as silently as he had appeared. Elara stood frozen, her heart pounding in her ears.

Who was he? And how much did he know?

As she gathered herself, she realized the game was far more dangerous than she had anticipated. The mask of deception was everywhere, and the shadows that surrounded the duke's estate were closing in fast.

And Elara was no longer certain she would survive what came next.

5

Beneath the Silence

The cold air bit at Elara's skin as she hurried back through the estate's narrow corridors, her mind racing with fear and uncertainty. The man's threat still echoed in her ears, chilling her to the core. She didn't recognize him, but his words—his warning—made it clear that someone knew about her involvement. She had only just started, yet already the walls were closing in.

She reached the door to her chambers and slipped inside, locking it behind her. Leaning against the wood, she tried to steady her breath. The estate was full of eyes and ears, and any wrong move could be her last. She couldn't stay here, not after what had just happened. But where could she go? Ryland would know what to do—he had to. He understood this world better than anyone, and she had no other allies she could trust.

Crossing the room quickly, she opened the drawer of her vanity and pulled out a small slip of parchment. Her hands shook as she scribbled a hurried note to Ryland, arranging a meeting near the old stables at dusk. It was the only place they could speak without fear of being overheard. She sealed the note and rang for her maid, handing it to her with a stern instruction to deliver it discreetly.

As soon as the maid left, Elara moved to the window. The estate grounds were sprawling, with gardens, stables, and the thick forest that bordered the property. From her vantage point, she could see the distant figures of guards patrolling along the perimeter. Everything looked peaceful, yet beneath that silence, danger lurked, waiting for her to make a mistake.

The hours dragged by painfully. Elara kept her door locked, her heart leaping at every small sound from the hallway outside. She felt like a prisoner in her own room, trapped between the weight of her discovery and the threats looming around her. Her mind kept drifting back to the masked figure, his voice dripping with menace. Was he one of the conspirators Ryland had warned her about? Or had someone else learned of her snooping?

Dusk finally came, and with it, her opportunity to slip away unnoticed. Draping herself in a dark cloak, she left her chambers and made her way through the quiet corridors. Servants were busy preparing for the ball that would begin in just a few hours, giving her enough cover to move unseen.

When she reached the rear of the estate, she took a narrow servant's staircase down to the grounds. Her heart pounded in her chest as she stepped out into the fading light. The stables were a short distance away, nestled against the edge of the forest. She moved quickly, keeping to the shadows, her eyes darting around for any sign of movement.

As she neared the stables, she saw a figure standing just outside, partially hidden in the gloom. She froze, but then recognized Ryland's silhouette. Relief washed over her, and she hurried forward, her boots crunching softly against the gravel.

"Ryland," she called in a low voice, her breath misting in the evening air.

He turned at the sound of her voice, his face partially obscured by the darkness, but his eyes gleamed in the dim light. "You're late," he said, though there was no irritation in his tone, only concern.

"I had to be careful," Elara replied, stepping closer. She glanced around nervously before lowering her voice. "I was followed today. A man—he confronted me in one of the corridors. He warned me to stop, to stay out of this."

Ryland's expression darkened, his jaw tightening. "What did he look like?"

"He was tall, wearing a cloak... his face was mostly hidden. But his voice—it was cold, and he knew what I was doing. He knew I was investigating."

Ryland cursed under his breath, pacing for a moment before stopping in front of her. "That means we're closer than I thought. Someone must be getting nervous, which means we're on the right trail. But it also means you're in more danger than ever."

Elara swallowed, the weight of his words settling heavily on her. "What do we do now?"

Ryland was silent for a moment, his eyes scanning the surrounding trees as if searching for hidden eyes watching them. Finally, he turned back to her, his voice low and urgent. "There's no going back. If they know you're involved, they won't stop until you're silenced—permanently. We need to push forward, but we have to be smart. The ball tonight is our best chance."

Elara's heart skipped a beat. "The ball? But how—?"

"Everyone will be there. It's the perfect opportunity to observe, to see who's aligning with whom. People let their guard down when they think they're safe, especially at events like this. We'll need to be subtle, but if we watch carefully, we might be able to identify who's behind this."

Elara nodded, though fear still gnawed at the edges of her resolve. She had never been involved in anything like this—plots, betrayals, life-or-death stakes. But there was no turning back now. Too much was at risk, and the longer the conspiracy remained hidden, the closer the duke came to falling into its trap.

Ryland reached into his coat and pulled out a folded piece of parchment. "This is a list of everyone who will be at the ball tonight, including those from the inner circle. Study it carefully. If we're lucky, we might catch something—an odd look, a secret conversation. But stay close to me. If anything feels wrong, we leave. Understood?"

Elara took the parchment, her fingers trembling slightly as she tucked it into her cloak. "Understood."

They stood in silence for a moment, the night pressing in around them, thick with unspoken tension. Ryland's hand brushed against her arm, a brief but reassuring gesture that sent a flicker of warmth through her amidst the cold fear gripping her heart.

"Be careful, Elara," he said quietly. "We're walking a fine line, and one wrong step could cost us everything."

Elara nodded, meeting his gaze. "I know. But I'm ready."

As they parted ways, slipping back into the shadows, Elara couldn't shake the feeling that they were being watched, that unseen eyes were tracking their every move. The silence of the night was too still, too quiet, as if something sinister waited just beyond the edge of the light.

And as the moon rose higher, casting long, eerie shadows across the estate, Elara knew that tonight would change everything.

6

Shadows in the Ballroom

The ballroom shimmered with opulence, its high ceilings adorned with glittering chandeliers, and the walls draped in rich tapestries of crimson and gold. The grand event had drawn in the finest of the duke's court, each guest clad in lavish gowns and tailored suits, their laughter and conversation filling the air with a false sense of merriment. Yet, beneath the surface, Elara could feel the tension, the subtle undercurrent of suspicion that wound its way through the crowd.

She stood at the edge of the room, her heart racing as she surveyed the scene before her. Ryland's instructions echoed in her mind—observe, but stay quiet. The conspirators were here, hidden among the guests, and if they slipped up, even for a moment, Elara had to be ready.

Her fingers brushed against the parchment still hidden in her cloak, the list Ryland had given her of the key players attending tonight. She had memorized the names, faces, and affiliations, though it did little to quell the anxiety gnawing at her. Lady Margot was there, as radiant and calculating as ever, her emerald gown shimmering in the candlelight as she charmed those around her. The duke, regal and stoic, held court in the center of the room, his sharp eyes scanning the guests with practiced disinterest.

And then there were the others—the shadowy figures that had been circling the court for months, their loyalties uncertain. Elara's gaze flicked to one such figure, Lord Alistair, standing near the far corner, his dark eyes watching the crowd with a predator's gaze. His reputation was one of cunning and ruthlessness, his alliances shifting like the wind. Could he be the one plotting against the duke? Or was he just another viper in the nest?

"Elara."

Ryland's voice at her side startled her, and she turned to find him standing close, his expression unreadable. He had slipped into the ballroom unnoticed, his presence as shadowed as the secrets he carried. He wore a simple black suit, nothing flashy, but the way he held himself commanded attention. His eyes, sharp and observant, swept over the room before settling on her.

"Any signs?" he asked in a low voice, his gaze not leaving the crowd.

Elara shook her head, her voice tight. "Nothing yet. But everyone's here. If they're going to make a move, it has to be soon."

Ryland nodded, his jaw tightening. "Keep watching. Stay close to the duke if you can, but don't draw attention to yourself. We need to be ready for anything."

Elara gave a small nod and watched as Ryland melted back into the crowd, his movements as fluid as ever. She envied his ability to blend in so effortlessly, while every step she took felt heavy with the weight of her mission. The music swelled, a lively waltz filling the room as couples began to take to the dance floor.

She moved carefully, weaving her way through the throng of guests, her eyes constantly shifting, looking for anything out of place. As she neared the duke, she caught sight of something—an interaction, brief but suspicious. A man, dressed in the livery of a servant, handed a note to Lord Alistair. The lord glanced around quickly before tucking the note into his jacket, his face betraying nothing.

Elara's heart skipped a beat. Was this it? Was the conspiracy unfolding right in front of her?

She edged closer, trying to get a better view, but the swell of dancers blocked her line of sight. Frustrated, she moved to the side of the room, hoping for a clearer vantage point. But before she could take another step, a hand clamped down on her wrist.

"Careful, my lady," a smooth voice whispered in her ear.

Elara froze, her pulse skyrocketing as she turned to face the man who had grabbed her. It was him—the hooded figure from the corridor. He was dressed now as a nobleman, his face fully visible, but the cold menace in his eyes was unmistakable. His grip tightened just enough to send a warning.

"You're meddling in things that don't concern you," he murmured, his breath hot against her skin. "You should have listened."

Elara's throat went dry, fear clawing at her as she tried to pull her wrist free. "Let go of me," she hissed, trying to keep her voice steady.

The man's lips curled into a smile, but it didn't reach his eyes. "You've made your choice. Now you'll face the consequences."

He released her wrist abruptly, stepping back into the crowd as if nothing had happened. Elara stood frozen, her heart pounding in her chest, her wrist still tingling from his touch. She glanced around, but the ballroom carried on as if the encounter had never occurred. No one had seen, no one had noticed.

But Ryland had warned her. The conspiracy ran deep, and now she was caught in its web.

She forced herself to move, her feet carrying her toward the duke, who was now engaged in conversation with several of his advisors. Elara's mind raced, her thoughts tumbling over one another. She had to warn him. She had to do something before it was too late. But how? If she approached the duke directly, she risked exposing herself, and the conspirators were already watching her every move.

As she neared the duke's group, her eyes caught sight of something that made her blood run cold. A servant approached the duke with a tray of wine, but as he handed the goblet to the duke, his hand trembled ever so slightly. It was a tiny movement, almost imperceptible—but to Elara, it was a warning. She had seen that servant before, in the corridor where she had been threatened.

Her heart slammed against her ribs. The wine. It had to be poisoned.

Without thinking, she rushed forward, her hand shooting out to knock the goblet from the duke's grasp. The wine spilled across the floor, the delicate glass shattering on impact. Gasps rippled through the crowd as heads turned toward the commotion.

"Elara!" The duke's voice was sharp, his eyes narrowing in confusion and anger. "What is the meaning of this?"

But before she could answer, the servant bolted. Ryland, moving faster than anyone else in the room, darted after him. Chaos erupted, the guests murmuring in confusion as the pieces began to fall into place. Elara's heart raced as she realized the full extent of what had just happened.

The trap had been set. And she had just sprung it.

7

The Poisoned Truth

The ballroom had descended into chaos. Elara stood frozen for a moment, the shattered goblet at her feet and the shocked faces of the crowd swirling around her. The duke's angry voice still echoed in her ears, but it was drowned out by the pounding of her heart. She had just disrupted the evening's most critical moment, and now all eyes were on her.

"Elara," the duke repeated, his voice steely as he took a step toward her, his face a mask of controlled fury. "Explain yourself."

Her throat was dry, and for a moment, words failed her. She opened her mouth, but before she could speak, Ryland returned. He moved with quiet authority, his hand clamped firmly around the arm of the fleeing servant, now dragged back into the ballroom. The man's face was pale, his eyes wide with fear as Ryland pushed him toward the center of the room.

"This man," Ryland said loudly, his voice cutting through the low murmurs of the crowd, "was about to serve Your Grace a poisoned drink."

A ripple of shock swept through the room. Elara felt the weight of countless eyes on her, their suspicion and confusion palpable. The duke's gaze, however, remained fixed on her, his brow furrowed in anger and disbelief.

"A poisoned drink?" The duke's voice was cold, his eyes narrowing as he glanced at the servant now trembling under Ryland's grip. "And you, Elara, knew this how?"

Elara swallowed hard, her pulse racing. She had no clear answer, no solid proof, only instincts and fleeting suspicions. The room seemed to close in around her, the walls pressing in tighter as the silence stretched.

"I—" she started, her voice barely above a whisper. "I noticed something off about him earlier. He's been following me, watching me. When I saw him hand you the wine, I knew something was wrong."

The duke's frown deepened, but before he could respond, Ryland stepped forward. "Your Grace, I can vouch for Lady Elara's instincts. I've been investigating a growing conspiracy against you. This man," he gestured to the servant, "is part of it."

The crowd gasped again, their whispers growing louder, a current of disbelief and fear threading through the room. The duke's eyes flicked from Ryland to the servant, then back to Elara, the weight of his scrutiny pressing down on her.

"And you," the duke said to the servant, his voice deadly calm, "do you deny this?"

The servant trembled visibly now, his face slick with sweat. He shook his head, his voice barely a croak. "I—I didn't mean to! I was just following orders!"

"Whose orders?" Ryland demanded, his grip tightening on the man's arm.

The servant's eyes darted around the room, searching for some form of escape, but there was none. The crowd had gathered close, their eyes hungry for answers, for blood. His lips quivered as he stammered, "It—it was Lord Alistair! He—he paid me! I swear, I was only doing what he said!"

A collective gasp rose from the crowd as all eyes turned to Lord Alistair, standing at the far end of the room. The nobleman's face was an unreadable mask, his dark eyes cold and calculating. He made no move to speak, no denial, no defense. His silence sent a chill through the room.

The duke's expression darkened, his gaze locking onto Lord Alistair. "Is this true?" he asked, his voice quiet but laced with steel.

For a moment, no one spoke. The tension was thick enough to cut, the air crackling with anticipation. Then, with a slow, deliberate motion, Lord Alistair took a step forward, his eyes gleaming with something dark and unreadable.

"And if it were true?" Alistair's voice was low, dangerous. "Would it surprise you, Your Grace, to learn that not everyone in your court is as loyal as they seem?"

The room froze. Every breath held, every pair of eyes locked on the unfolding confrontation. Elara's heart raced as she realized the full weight of what was happening. This wasn't just about poison or one servant's betrayal. This was a rebellion, simmering beneath the surface for longer than anyone had realized.

The duke's face hardened, his hand instinctively moving to the hilt of the ceremonial sword at his waist. "Are you confessing, Alistair?"

Lord Alistair smirked, a cold and dangerous smile. "I'm simply saying, Your Grace, that perhaps you should have paid more attention to those you've surrounded yourself with. The truth has been in front of you all along—you've just been too blind to see it."

A ripple of unease moved through the crowd. Some guests shifted nervously, others glanced toward the exits, but no one moved. The air was thick with the threat of violence, as if the tension could snap at any moment.

Ryland's hand twitched toward the dagger hidden beneath his coat, his eyes never leaving Alistair. "Enough with the riddles. Either you're involved in this plot or you're not."

Alistair's smile faded, replaced by a cold, calculating glare. "The truth is, Ryland, there are many involved in this. Far more than you could ever know. You and your little spy here," he shot a glance at Elara, "are far too late to stop what's coming."

Elara's blood ran cold. It wasn't just Lord Alistair. This went deeper—far deeper than she or Ryland had anticipated. She had thought they were uncovering a conspiracy, but in truth, they had only scratched the surface.

The duke, his face now a mask of fury, took a step toward Alistair, his voice low and commanding. "I will have you hanged for this treachery, Alistair. Whatever plot you're involved in ends tonight."

But Alistair merely laughed, a hollow, chilling sound that echoed through the ballroom. "You think you can stop this, Your Grace? This is beyond you. The wheels are already in motion. By the time you realize what's happening, it will be far too late."

Suddenly, the doors to the ballroom burst open, and several guards rushed in, their faces pale with panic. "Your Grace!" one of them shouted, breathless. "There's been an attack—on the northern watchtower. The estate is under siege!"

Chaos erupted. The guests scattered, panicked cries filling the room as the realization dawned. This wasn't just a plot. This was a coup.

Elara's heart raced, her mind spinning as she tried to process what was happening. Ryland moved to her side, his expression grim. "We need to get the duke to safety. Now."

As the ballroom dissolved into chaos, Elara knew one thing for certain: the shadows that had been lurking at the edges of the duke's court were no longer content to stay hidden. They had come for blood. And there would be no escape.

8

The Flames of Betrayal

The panic in the ballroom was like a living beast, its claws tearing through the walls of the grand hall as the guests rushed for the exits. Elara's heartbeat hammered in her chest, the sound deafening in her ears as she struggled to make sense of the chaos unfolding before her. The guards' warning replayed in her mind—the estate is under siege. She felt Ryland's hand grip her arm tightly, pulling her from her daze as the world around them seemed to implode.

"Move!" Ryland's voice cut through the noise, firm and commanding. "We need to get the duke out of here now."

Elara nodded, her throat tight as she forced her legs to move. The room was a storm of panicked nobles, fleeing in all directions like scattered leaves. She could barely make out faces through the frenzy of movement, but the one that stood out, chilling her to her bones, was Lord Alistair. He hadn't moved from where he stood at the far end of the ballroom, his cold smile still playing on his lips as if he were a spectator enjoying the chaos he had orchestrated.

The duke, surrounded by his closest advisors, barked orders at the guards who had rushed in. But it was clear even to Elara that they were outnumbered. The northern watchtower had already fallen, and the enemy—whoever they were—was closing in. Ryland's grip on her arm tightened as they approached the duke, his eyes scanning the exits with the practiced vigilance of a man who had been in dangerous situations too many times before.

"Your Grace," Ryland said urgently, addressing the duke. "We need to get you to safety. There's no time."

The duke, still gripping the hilt of his sword, looked at Ryland with cold fury. "You expect me to run, Ryland? I will not abandon my estate to a pack of traitors."

Elara could see the anger in the duke's eyes, but there was something else there too—fear, barely hidden beneath his composed exterior. He didn't want to flee, but he knew as well as anyone that staying would mean certain death.

"Your Grace," Elara cut in, her voice shaking slightly but firm, "you won't be abandoning anything. If you stay here, they'll kill you. You need to live to fight another day."

The duke's eyes flicked to her, and for a moment, she thought he might lash out in anger. But then, something in his expression shifted. He nodded, though begrudgingly. "Very well. But we leave through the southern passage. It leads to the forest. We can regroup at the hunter's lodge there."

Ryland didn't waste a moment. He gestured toward a side door, hidden behind a tapestry, and signaled to the guards. "Stay close," he ordered Elara, his voice barely above a whisper.

As they moved toward the door, Elara felt a cold prickle run down her spine. She glanced back over her shoulder, her eyes scanning the ballroom one last time. Lord Alistair was still standing there, his gaze locked onto her with an intensity that made her blood run cold. He didn't move, didn't say a word, but his expression told her everything she needed to know. This wasn't over—not by a long shot.

The small group made their way through the passage, the air growing cooler as the stone walls closed in around them. The sound of chaos from the ballroom faded into the distance, replaced by the echo of their hurried footsteps. Elara's heart pounded in her chest, her mind racing as they descended deeper into the estate's hidden corridors. The southern passage was rarely used, a secret known only to a few. If they could make it to the forest, they might have a chance.

But just as that thought passed through her mind, a loud crash echoed from ahead, followed by the sound of metal clashing against stone. Elara's breath hitched in her throat as they skidded to a stop.

"What was that?" one of the guards asked, his hand already on the hilt of his sword.

Ryland held up a hand, his eyes narrowing as he moved cautiously forward. "Stay behind me."

Elara's heart thundered in her ears as they crept down the passage. The air was thick with tension, every sound amplified in the narrow space. They rounded a corner, and there—blocking their path—were two armed men, dressed in black and bearing the unmistakable insignia of the traitors.

Before anyone could react, Ryland lunged forward, drawing his dagger with deadly precision. The first man barely had time to raise his sword before Ryland's blade found its mark, sinking into his throat with a sickening crunch. The second attacker charged, but the guards rushed to meet him, swords clashing violently as the narrow passage filled with the sounds of battle.

Elara's breath caught in her chest as she backed away, her eyes wide with fear. The passage was too small for her to run without risking a confrontation, and she had no weapon. She pressed herself against the cold stone wall, her heart hammering as the fight unfolded before her. Ryland fought like a man possessed, his movements swift and deadly, but even he couldn't fight forever.

Just as the second attacker was brought down by one of the duke's guards, Elara heard a sound behind her—a low, quiet whisper of fabric brushing against stone. She turned, and her blood ran cold.

Another figure emerged from the shadows, his eyes gleaming with malevolent intent. He moved silently, a dagger glinting in his hand as he approached the duke from behind.

Without thinking, Elara lunged forward, her hands grabbing the only weapon she could find—a fallen guard's sword. It was heavy, and her grip was unsteady, but she didn't have time to second-guess herself. The assassin's blade was already descending toward the duke's unprotected back.

With a cry that was more instinct than thought, Elara swung the sword with all her strength. The blade collided with the assassin's arm, knocking the dagger from his grasp just inches from the duke's throat. The man snarled in pain, spinning to face her, but before he could react, Ryland was there. His dagger flashed through the air, catching the would-be killer in the chest.

The assassin crumpled to the floor, dead before he hit the ground.

For a moment, silence filled the passage, broken only by the sound of Elara's ragged breathing. She stared down at the body, the reality of what had just happened sinking in. She had saved the duke's life. But as her gaze lifted to meet Ryland's, she saw no relief in his eyes.

"There will be more," he said quietly, his voice laced with grim certainty. "We're not safe yet."

And as they moved deeper into the shadows of the southern passage, Elara knew that the worst was still to come.

9

The Forest of Deceit

The narrow corridor twisted and turned, the dim light flickering from the torches on the walls as Elara followed Ryland and the duke deeper into the estate's hidden passageways. Every footfall echoed ominously, a constant reminder of the danger lurking just behind them. The air was thick with the scent of damp earth and stone, and Elara could feel the cold seeping into her bones. It was hard to believe that only hours ago, the ballroom had been alive with laughter and music, a world away from this claustrophobic nightmare.

As they reached the end of the corridor, they pushed through a heavy wooden door that led to the outside. The cool night air rushed in, carrying with it the scent of pine and the distant sounds of chaos—the shouts of guards, the clashing of swords, and the crackle of flames. The estate was under siege, and the reality of their situation settled heavily in Elara's chest.

"Quickly!" Ryland urged, his eyes scanning the trees lining the edge of the estate. "We need to get to the woods. There's a hunter's lodge not far from here; we can regroup and plan our next move."

Elara nodded, her breath coming in quick bursts as they raced into the darkness. The trees loomed like sentinels, their branches whispering secrets as the wind wove through them. The moon hung low in the sky, casting an ethereal glow that barely penetrated the thick canopy. Elara kept close to Ryland, her heart pounding in her ears, the sounds of the battle behind them growing fainter.

They moved with urgency, the weight of their mission pressing down on them. The duke remained silent, his jaw clenched as he led the way, a mix of determination and vulnerability etched across his face. Elara couldn't help but glance back, half-expecting to see shadows emerging from the estate, figures cloaked in darkness ready to pursue them. But for now, they seemed to have evaded the worst.

As they plunged deeper into the woods, the sounds of the battle faded, replaced by the rustling of leaves and the distant hoot of an owl. Elara struggled to catch her breath, trying to push down the fear that threatened to consume her. They had survived the ballroom, but the danger was far from over. She couldn't shake the feeling that they were being watched, the forest itself alive with unseen eyes.

"Here," Ryland whispered, gesturing to a small clearing where a dilapidated cabin stood, partially hidden by overgrown foliage. It looked abandoned, but it was their best option. The duke nodded, and they moved quickly toward the structure, their footsteps muffled by the carpet of pine needles beneath them.

Inside, the air was stale, filled with the scent of damp wood and decay. The cabin was sparse—just a table, some broken chairs, and a fireplace lined with ash. Ryland moved to the window, peering out into the darkness, while the duke took a seat on the table, his shoulders slumped.

"What do we do now?" Elara asked, her voice barely above a whisper as she joined the duke.

"We regroup," the duke replied, his tone steely. "We need to understand what we're up against and devise a plan to counter it."

Ryland turned from the window, his expression serious. "We know Alistair is involved, and there are others we haven't accounted for. We need to find out who they are and what their objectives are."

Elara felt a chill run down her spine. "What if they're already searching for us?"

The duke's gaze hardened. "Then we'll have to outsmart them. They may have the advantage of surprise, but we have the element of secrecy. We know these woods better than they do."

The tension in the room was palpable, the weight of their predicament hanging over them like a shroud. Elara could sense the duke's determination, but there was also a flicker of fear in his eyes. He was a ruler facing betrayal from within, and she could only imagine the burden of that reality.

Suddenly, the crack of a branch echoed from outside, making them all freeze. Ryland's hand went to his dagger, and he gestured for silence. The three of them stood still, listening intently as footsteps crunched on the forest floor, drawing closer.

"Stay low," Ryland whispered, positioning himself near the door.

Elara's heart raced as she crouched beside the table, her eyes fixed on the door. She felt a rush of adrenaline, a mixture of fear and resolve surging through her veins. Whoever was out there could very well be their pursuers, and she was determined to protect the duke, no matter the cost.

The footsteps stopped just outside the door, and Elara held her breath, every muscle in her body tense. They waited in silence, the air thick with anticipation. And then, the door creaked open, slowly revealing a silhouette framed by the moonlight.

"Ryland? Elara?" The voice was familiar—Tobias, one of the duke's loyal guards. Relief washed over Elara as he stepped inside, his expression a mix of urgency and concern.

"Thank the stars," Tobias said, his voice low but urgent. "I thought I'd lost you all."

"What's happening?" Ryland demanded, his body relaxing slightly as he recognized his friend.

"We're being overwhelmed. Alistair's forces have spread through the estate, and they're gaining ground. We've lost contact with several patrols, and the northern watchtower is entirely compromised," Tobias reported, his brow furrowed in worry. "We need to leave this place and regroup elsewhere. They're already searching the woods for anyone who escaped."

The duke's face hardened. "We can't run forever. We need to make a stand."

"No," Tobias said firmly, shaking his head. "We need to gather as many loyal men as we can and fortify our position. The hunter's lodge is too exposed. We should move to the caves beyond the ridge. It's an old hideout used by hunters—hidden from sight and easy to defend."

Elara exchanged a glance with Ryland. "The caves?"

"Yes," Tobias insisted. "We can plan our next move from there. It's the safest option right now, and we can find a way to strike back against Alistair. But we need to go now, while we still have the chance."

The urgency of his words ignited something in Elara. They couldn't afford to be scared; they had to act. "Let's do it," she said, her voice steady. "We can't let Alistair win. We need to fight back."

The duke nodded, his eyes fierce with determination. "Very well. Tobias, lead the way. We'll follow close behind."

As they moved out of the cabin, Elara felt a flicker of hope spark within her. The night was dark and dangerous, but they were not alone. They had allies, and together, they would confront the betrayal that had threatened to tear them apart. With every step they took into the shadows, she felt the weight of the battle ahead, but she also felt a growing strength, a resolve to fight for the life and future they all believed in.

But as they slipped into the darkness of the forest, the feeling of being watched returned, a chilling reminder that they were not the only ones lurking among the trees. And Elara knew that with every choice they made, they were drawing closer to a confrontation that would either seal their fate or grant them the victory they desperately sought.

10

The Echoes of Betrayal

The moon hung high in the night sky, its pale light struggling to penetrate the dense canopy of leaves overhead. As Elara, Ryland, the duke, and Tobias moved silently through the underbrush, every snap of a twig felt like a gunshot in the stillness of the forest. They kept to the shadows, navigating the familiar terrain with caution, knowing that every step brought them closer to the heart of their enemies.

Elara's mind raced as she replayed the events of the past few hours. They had barely escaped the estate, and now they were deep in the woods, where danger lurked around every corner. Alistair's forces were out there, hunting them, and they had to be careful not to draw attention to themselves. The weight of the moment pressed heavily on her, and she struggled to shake the feeling of dread that clung to her.

"Stay close," Ryland whispered, glancing back at Elara, his expression tight with focus. "We're almost at the ridge. Keep your eyes open."

Elara nodded, her heart pounding as they continued to move forward. The further they ventured into the forest, the more her instincts screamed at her to be wary. The shadows danced around them, and she couldn't shake the feeling that they were not alone.

As they climbed the ridge, the air grew cooler, and the scent of damp earth and moss enveloped them. Elara led the way, her senses heightened, every sound amplifying in the silence. They reached a rocky outcrop that overlooked the valley below. The view was breathtaking, but Elara barely noticed. She could see the faint glow of flames in the distance, evidence of the chaos that had erupted at the estate.

"From here, we can see if any of Alistair's men are patrolling the area," Tobias said, positioning himself at the edge of the outcrop. The duke joined him, and together, they scanned the surroundings.

"Is it safe to move?" the duke asked, his voice low and filled with concern.

"I don't see anyone yet," Tobias replied, but there was a note of caution in his tone. "We should make our way down to the caves quickly, though. The longer we stay exposed, the greater the risk."

Ryland turned to Elara, his eyes searching hers. "Are you ready for this?"

Elara nodded, steeling herself for what lay ahead. "We need to keep moving. We can't afford to be caught out here."

With a silent agreement, they began their descent, carefully navigating the rocky terrain. As they moved, the weight of uncertainty hung in the air. They were so close to safety, yet every instinct told Elara that something was wrong. A nagging feeling of being watched followed her, a whisper of danger lurking just beyond their line of sight.

Once they reached the cave entrance, they stepped inside, the darkness enveloping them like a heavy shroud. The interior was cool and damp, the sound of dripping water echoing off the walls. Elara felt a chill run down her spine, the silence inside the cave pressing in on her.

Tobias lit a small lantern, casting flickering shadows across the rough stone walls. They gathered in a small clearing, their faces illuminated by the warm glow. The atmosphere shifted, and Elara could sense the tension building as they began to strategize.

"We can fortify the entrance and set traps," Tobias suggested, his voice steady. "If Alistair's men find us, we'll need every advantage we can get."

"And we need to find allies," Ryland added, his expression resolute. "We can't take on Alistair alone. We need to rally the loyalists who have not yet fallen under his sway."

The duke nodded, his face serious. "We'll send scouts out to gather information. If we can learn how many men Alistair has, it will help us formulate a plan. But we need to be careful. They will be looking for us, and if they find us before we're ready, it could be the end."

Elara listened intently, her mind racing as they discussed their next steps. She wanted to contribute, to be more than just a bystander in this fight, but fear coursed through her veins, making her hesitate.

"What if we can't find enough support?" she asked, her voice shaking slightly. "What if Alistair is stronger than we anticipate?"

"Then we'll fight anyway," Ryland replied, his gaze fierce. "We've already lost too much. We can't back down now."

Determination flickered within Elara, but it was tempered by the weight of reality. They were facing not just a physical battle but a war of wits against a man who had already betrayed them once. Alistair was cunning, and she knew that underestimating him would be a grave mistake.

Just as they were discussing their options, a faint sound echoed from deeper within the cave—a soft scraping noise, like something dragging across the stone floor. Elara's heart stopped, and she exchanged worried glances with the others.

"Did you hear that?" she whispered, her voice barely audible.

The group fell silent, straining to listen. The sound grew louder, a shuffling that echoed ominously through the darkness. Ryland moved toward the entrance, his dagger drawn, while the duke and Tobias positioned themselves protectively around Elara.

The shadows danced on the walls as the sound grew closer. Elara held her breath, her heart racing as a figure emerged from the darkness. It was another guard—one of their own—his face pale and covered in dirt.

"Help…me," he gasped, stumbling into the light. His clothes were torn, and his eyes were wild with fear. "They're coming. Alistair's men…they found me."

"What happened?" Ryland demanded, moving closer.

"I was scouting ahead when they caught me," the guard said, trembling. "There's a whole battalion moving through the woods. They're searching for you. I barely escaped. We have to get out of here!"

Elara's stomach dropped at the guard's words. They were running out of time, and Alistair was closing in. They needed a plan, and fast.

"Gather your weapons," the duke ordered, his voice firm. "We can't stay here. If Alistair's men are near, we need to move and find a safer location. We'll head deeper into the caves where they won't find us."

As the others began to prepare, Elara felt a sense of urgency surging within her. She had faced danger before, but this was different. This was a fight for their lives, and she refused to let fear dictate her actions.

"Ryland," she called, catching his attention. "What if we set a trap here? We could use the cave's entrance to our advantage. If we can draw them in, we might be able to take some of them out."

He paused, considering her suggestion. "It's risky, but it might just work. If we can lure them into the open, we can fight them on our terms."

"Let's do it," Elara said, her determination shining through the fear that gripped her.

With a newfound sense of purpose, they began to devise a plan, using the cave's natural features to their advantage. They worked quickly, adrenaline fueling their movements as they prepared for the inevitable confrontation.

But as they set their traps, Elara couldn't shake the feeling that the darkness around them was hiding more than just enemies. It felt alive, a twisting entity that could turn on them at any moment. The echo of betrayal loomed large, and Elara steeled herself for the fight ahead, knowing that every moment counted.

As they finished their preparations, a low rumble of voices echoed from outside the cave. The time for hiding was over. They would soon face Alistair's men, and with every heartbeat, Elara felt the weight of destiny pressing down upon her. She was no longer just a pawn in this game—she was ready to fight, and she would not back down.

Together, they waited in the darkness, hearts pounding, ready to confront whatever lay ahead. And as the first shadow fell across the entrance, Elara gripped her weapon tightly, ready to face the echoes of betrayal that had brought them all to this moment.

11

Shadows the Moonlight

The air was thick with the scent of pine and damp earth as Mia navigated the narrow trail, her heart racing with each step. The moon hung high in the sky, casting silvery beams that flickered like ghostly fingers through the canopy. Shadows danced around her, morphing into dark shapes that seemed to whisper secrets of the forest. She had lost track of time, her mind consumed by the events of the previous days and the truth she had unearthed about her family.

Mia had never believed in the supernatural; she had always grounded herself in reality. But now, as the trees closed in around her and the wind rustled through the leaves, she couldn't shake the feeling that something—no, someone—was watching her. The thought made her skin crawl.

Earlier that day, she had discovered an old journal belonging to her grandmother, hidden away in a dusty trunk in the attic. The pages were yellowed and brittle, filled with the delicate cursive of a woman who had lived through turbulent times. Mia's fingers trembled as she read the words detailing her grandmother's encounters with the mysterious figure known only as "The Keeper." According to the journal, The Keeper was a guardian of secrets, a spirit who roamed the woods, bestowing wisdom upon those brave enough to seek it. But the journal hinted at a darker side—a warning against seeking the Keeper's knowledge.

As Mia delved deeper into the journal's secrets, she came across a passage that chilled her to the bone: "Those who seek the truth often find themselves lost, their souls entwined with shadows. The Keeper is not to be trifled with."

Now, as the forest swallowed her in its embrace, Mia couldn't shake the feeling that she had stepped into a realm where the lines between reality and myth blurred. A sharp snap of a twig echoed behind her, causing her to spin around, heart pounding in her chest. "Hello?" she called out, her voice trembling slightly in the stillness. There was no response, only the rustle of leaves in the wind, the forest seeming to mock her bravery.

She took a cautious step forward, every instinct urging her to turn back. But curiosity propelled her deeper into the woods. She recalled her grandmother's stories of hidden clearings where the moonlight illuminated ancient symbols etched into the ground—symbols that whispered of lost knowledge and powerful magic. Mia's mind raced. What if she could find one of those clearings? What if she could uncover the truth behind her family's legacy?

The path twisted and turned, and soon Mia found herself standing at the edge of a small clearing. Moonlight poured down, illuminating a circle of stones arranged in a perfect ring, each stone covered in moss and age-old markings that glimmered with an otherworldly light. The air hummed with energy, an electric charge that sent shivers up her spine.

Mia stepped forward, entranced by the beauty of the stones. She knelt down, brushing her fingers over the symbols, feeling a strange warmth beneath her fingertips. As she traced the lines, a low rumble resonated in the ground beneath her, and she froze, her breath hitching in her throat. The forest seemed to hold its breath, and in that moment, she knew she wasn't alone.

Suddenly, a figure emerged from the shadows at the far edge of the clearing. Tall and cloaked in darkness, it moved with an unnatural grace, as if gliding rather than walking. Mia's heart raced as she squinted into the gloom, trying to discern the figure's features. It was then that she remembered the warnings from her grandmother's journal: "The Keeper will reveal themselves, but at a cost."

"Mia," a voice called out, smooth and resonant, echoing through the clearing. It was neither male nor female, but held an otherworldly quality that made the hair on her arms stand on end. "You seek answers, do you not?"

"I—yes," Mia stammered, her voice barely above a whisper. "Who are you?"

"I am The Keeper," the figure replied, stepping closer, the shadows shifting around it like living fabric. "I guard the secrets of your lineage, the truth that binds you to this land. But to uncover what you seek, you must be willing to confront the darkness within yourself."

A chill ran through Mia, the weight of those words pressing down on her chest. She thought of the journal, the secrets it held, and the fear that had gripped her heart since she began this journey. Could she truly face whatever darkness lurked within her family's past?

"What do I need to do?" she asked, her voice steadier now, fueled by determination.

The Keeper extended a hand, palm upturned, revealing a small, glimmering orb that pulsed with a soft light. "Take this. It holds the memories of those who came before you—their fears, their struggles, their triumphs. But beware, for knowledge comes at a price. Are you prepared to pay it?"

Mia hesitated, glancing back at the darkened path that had led her here. The choice hung heavily in the air. But in her heart, she knew there was no turning back. With trembling hands, she reached out, taking the orb in her grasp. As soon as her fingers wrapped around it, a rush of visions flooded her mind—faces she had never known, shadows of betrayal and love, echoes of laughter and tears.

The Keeper watched her, eyes glinting in the moonlight. "Now, you are bound to the truth. Embrace it, and the shadows shall guide you."

Mia felt a surge of power and fear collide within her, the forest around her alive with whispers of her ancestors. The journey had only just begun, and the path ahead was shrouded in darkness. But she would not falter. She would unravel the mystery of her lineage and confront the shadows that had haunted her family for generations. With the orb in her hand, Mia took a deep breath, ready to face whatever awaited her in the depths of the night.

12

The Heart of Darkness

The moon hung low in the sky, a silver sentinel overlooking the clearing where Mia stood, clutching the glowing orb that pulsed with an eerie light. The Keeper's presence loomed beside her, a shadow among shadows, waiting for her to respond to the weight of the knowledge she had just grasped. The air was thick with anticipation, every rustle of leaves and whisper of wind echoing the question that hung between them: What was she willing to sacrifice for the truth?

As Mia held the orb, images flooded her mind, vibrant and chaotic. She saw her grandmother, young and fierce, standing defiantly in the same clearing, a different orb in her hands, its light flickering like a dying star. The image shifted, revealing her grandmother's face, etched with sorrow and determination, as she whispered incantations into the night, calling forth the spirits of their ancestors.

"Mia," The Keeper's voice sliced through the torrent of visions, pulling her back to the present. "To understand your past, you must confront it. The orb reveals the truth, but it will also bring forth the shadows of your bloodline. Are you prepared?"

Mia nodded, her throat dry, resolve solidifying like a rock in her chest. "I have to know," she replied, her voice firmer than she felt. "I have to understand what my family has hidden."

The Keeper extended a hand, gesturing toward the stones surrounding them. "Place the orb at the center of the circle. It will awaken the spirits bound to this place."

Mia approached the center of the stone ring, heart pounding in her chest. The stones seemed to vibrate with energy, pulsing in rhythm with the orb in her hand. She took a deep breath, steadied herself, and set the orb down gently on the cold earth. As she withdrew her hand, a blinding light erupted from the orb, illuminating the clearing and casting long shadows against the trees.

The ground trembled beneath her feet, and the air crackled with energy. Mia felt a pull, as if the very essence of the forest was reaching for her, urging her to listen. The light swirled and danced, forming shapes that coalesced into figures—spectral forms of her ancestors, their faces twisted in expressions of anguish and hope.

"Child of the light," one of the figures spoke, a woman with long, flowing hair and eyes that glimmered like stars. "We are bound to this land, to the secrets you seek. Our stories are intertwined with yours."

Mia's heart raced. "What do I need to know?" she asked, her voice trembling. "What darkness have we harbored?"

The spirits began to swirl around her, their voices a cacophony of whispers. "The darkness came from within," another figure said, a man with a deep, resonant voice. "It was born from fear, betrayal, and the choices made by those who walked before you. It is a shadow that lingers, waiting to consume those who seek the truth without understanding."

Images flashed before her eyes—scenes of betrayal within her family, whispers of greed and ambition that led to the unraveling of bonds once thought unbreakable. She saw her grandmother standing alone, the weight of her family's sins heavy on her shoulders, desperately trying to protect the next generation from the darkness that threatened to engulf them.

"You have the power to break the cycle," the first woman said, her voice soothing yet commanding. "But you must confront the darkness head-on. Only then can you reclaim your family's legacy."

Mia swallowed hard, the weight of their words pressing down on her. "How do I confront it? What must I do?"

The spirits began to chant, their voices rising and falling like a haunting melody, weaving together a spell that resonated deep within her. The Keeper stepped closer, their shadow stretching long and ominous. "You must descend into the heart of the darkness, face the truth of your lineage, and make a choice that will define your path. The choice is not merely for you; it is for those who came before you and those who will follow."

The light from the orb began to dim, swirling into a vortex at the center of the clearing. Mia felt a pull, a gravitational force drawing her toward it. "You cannot shy away from what lies ahead," The Keeper urged. "You must go willingly into the depths."

Taking a deep breath, Mia stepped toward the vortex, feeling the warmth of the orb fading against her palm. The shadows around her twisted and morphed into swirling darkness, threatening to consume her. The forest around her felt alive, the trees creaking and groaning as if warning her to turn back. But she was resolute.

With one last glance at the spirits, their faces a mixture of hope and fear, Mia stepped into the vortex, surrendering to its pull. The world around her dissolved into a whirlwind of colors and sounds, blurring into a cacophony of memories and emotions.

When the chaos subsided, Mia found herself standing in a dimly lit cavern, the air thick with an ancient scent of earth and decay. Flickering torches lined the walls, casting eerie shadows that danced across the stone. In the center of the cavern stood an altar, dark and foreboding, stained with the echoes of past rituals and sacrifices.

She approached the altar cautiously, her heart racing. There, she saw it—a dark, twisted figure looming over the stone, its features obscured in shadow. "You've come," it hissed, a voice that slithered through the air like smoke. "The last of your bloodline. What do you seek?"

Mia's pulse quickened, every instinct screaming at her to flee. "I seek the truth," she managed to say, her voice steady despite the fear clawing at her throat. "I want to know what my family has hidden from me. I want to end the darkness."

The figure laughed, a chilling sound that echoed off the cavern walls. "To know the truth, you must embrace the darkness. You must choose to carry it, to wield it, or to destroy it. The choice will not come without sacrifice."

Mia took a step closer, determination solidifying in her heart. "I will not let the darkness consume me. I choose to destroy it."

The figure's expression twisted into a sneer. "You think you have the strength to end it? The darkness flows through your veins; it is a part of you. You cannot escape it!"

Mia felt a surge of energy within her, a fire igniting in her chest as she remembered the spirits of her ancestors, their voices encouraging her. "I am more than my bloodline," she shouted, raising her hands. "I am the culmination of every choice, every sacrifice, and I will not allow the darkness to define me!"

The cavern trembled, the shadows swirling violently as she summoned the light from the orb still clutched in her palm. It surged forth, illuminating the cavern and pushing back the shadows. The figure recoiled, its form flickering as Mia unleashed the light, a powerful force that filled the space with warmth and clarity.

With every ounce of her strength, she forced the darkness to retreat, the shadows writhing as they fought against the light. The cavern erupted in a blinding flash, the walls shaking as if the very foundation of the earth were splitting apart.

In that moment, Mia felt a connection with her ancestors, their spirits merging with hers, lending her strength. Together, they confronted the darkness, a collective force of will that shattered the shadows into fragments, scattering them into the void.

As the light enveloped her, Mia felt a profound sense of release, the weight of her family's sins lifting. The cavern began to crumble, the shadows dissipating, leaving behind an empty echo of what had once been.

And then, silence.

Mia opened her eyes, finding herself back in the clearing, the orb glowing softly at her feet. The spirits stood around her, their faces serene, their expressions filled with gratitude and peace. The Keeper nodded, a hint of approval in their gaze.

"You have done well, Mia," they said, their voice echoing in the stillness. "You have faced the darkness and emerged victorious. Your family's legacy is now free to grow anew."

As the first light of dawn broke over the horizon, Mia felt a sense of hope blooming within her. She had faced the shadows of her past and emerged stronger, ready to forge a new path, unencumbered by the weight of fear and secrecy.

With a deep breath, she turned to the forest, ready to embrace her future, her heart alight with the promise of new beginnings.

As the sun's first rays spilled over the horizon, bathing the clearing in a golden glow, Mia felt the warmth seep into her very soul. The spirits of her ancestors, once bound by darkness and regret, now radiated a serene light, their forms shimmering like reflections in water. She could sense their gratitude, the weight of their histories lifting with each passing moment.

"Thank you," she whispered, her voice barely audible above the gentle rustle of the leaves. "For guiding me, for helping me face the truth."

The spirits nodded, their eyes bright with an otherworldly light. "You are the bridge between past and future, Mia. Remember, the strength of your lineage lies not just in the blood that runs through your veins but in the choices you make and the light you carry forward."

Mia's heart swelled with a newfound purpose. She looked around the clearing, the ancient stones now glowing softly in the morning light, a reminder of the connection she shared with this land and the stories it held. The Keeper stepped forward, their presence reassuring, a shadow among the trees.

"Your journey is not over," they said, their voice a calming balm. "You have faced the darkness and emerged victorious, but the world still holds its challenges. Use the knowledge you've gained to forge a new path for yourself and your family. Share the stories, illuminate the shadows where others may linger."

Mia nodded, feeling the truth of those words resonate within her. She was ready to embrace the legacy of her family—not as a burden, but as a source of strength. "I will. I promise to honor our past and build a future filled with light."

With that, the spirits began to fade, their forms dissolving into the morning mist, leaving behind an ethereal sense of peace. The Keeper remained a moment longer, a silent guardian, before they too stepped back into the forest's embrace.

As the last traces of night slipped away, Mia felt the cool breeze brush against her skin, a gentle reminder that she was alive, that she had fought for her truth and won. The forest was alive with the sounds of morning—birds chirping, leaves rustling, the world awakening around her.

Mia knelt by the orb, still glowing softly on the ground. She picked it up, feeling its warmth spread through her palm. It was a symbol of her journey, a tangible reminder of her connection to her ancestors and the battles she had faced.

With one final glance at the clearing, she turned and began her walk back through the forest, the path clear before her. Each step felt lighter, the shadows of her past no longer clinging to her like a shroud but instead transforming into a guiding light that illuminated her way forward.

As she emerged from the trees, the sun rose higher in the sky, casting its radiant glow over the landscape. Mia felt an overwhelming sense of hope and possibility. She would return home and share her story, not only of the darkness that had threatened to consume her family but of the strength that emerged from confronting it.

In that moment, she knew her journey was just beginning. There would be challenges ahead, but she was equipped with the wisdom of her ancestors, the light of truth, and a heart ready to embrace whatever came next.

Mia smiled, a deep sense of peace settling within her as she stepped into the warmth of the new day, ready to forge her own path, unafraid of the shadows, knowing they would always be a part of her story but never again her master. The future awaited, bright and full of promise, and she was ready to meet it head-on.